Cultural Traditions in the

Netherlands

Kelly Spence

Crabtree Publishing Company
www.crabtreebooks.com

Crabtree Publishing Company
www.crabtreebooks.com

Author: Kelly Spence

Publishing plan research and development:
Reagan Miller

Editorial director: Kathy Middleton

Editors: Janine Deschenes, Crystal Sikkens

Proofreader and indexer: Petrice Custance

Photo research: Kelly Spence, Tammy McGarr

Designer: Tammy McGarr

Production coordinator and prepress technician:
Tammy McGarr

Print coordinator: Katherine Berti

Cover: Van Gogh's *Starry Night* (top); Street scene and canal in Amsterdam (background); Gouda cheese (bottom right); Oliebollen (bottom right); Dutch clogs or klompen (bottom left); Tulips (left); Festival dancers pose after traditional mother-daughter dance (center)

Title page: Girl holding tulips, the unofficial national flower of the Netherlands. In background, windmill and flowers in the Dutch countryside.

Photographs:
Alamy: © epa european pressphoto agency b.v.: p13 (middle right); © ZUMA Press, Inc.: p18; © Robert Hoetink: p19; © Peter Horree: p21 (top left);
AP Images: Peter Dejong: p14
Colourbox: Jan Sluimer: p23
Creative Commons: H. Zell: p6; Alexander Fritze: p9; Kang-min Liu: p10 (bottom); Hazelares: p13 (top left)
Dreamstime: © Claraveritas: p15 (bottom right);
iStock: © Doctor_bass: p7 (bottom); © VLIET: p17 (bottom); © thehague: p25 (top)
Public Domain: front cover (top); p22
Shutterstock: © Susan Montgomery: cover (center); © Tim Wong Amsterdam: p10 (inset); © Colette3: p11; © hans engbers: p12; © Cloud Mine Amsterdam: p16; © jan kranendonk: p24; © jan kranendonk: p28;
Superstock: Peter Willi: p26
Thinkstock: sharifphoto: cover (bottom right)
Wikimedia Commons: nl:Afbeelding:Sintmaarten: p27

All other images by Shutterstock

Library and Archives Canada Cataloguing in Publication

Spence, Kelly, author
    Cultural traditions in the Netherlands / Kelly Spence.

(Cultural traditions in my world)
Includes index.
Issued in print and electronic formats.
ISBN 978-0-7787-8089-2 (bound).--ISBN 978-0-7787-8093-9 (paperback).--ISBN 978-1-4271-8095-7 (html)

    1. Festivals--Netherlands--Juvenile literature. 2. Holidays--Netherlands--Juvenile literature. 3. Netherlands--Social life and customs--Juvenile literature. 4. Netherlands--Civilization--Juvenile literature.
I. Title. II. Series: Cultural traditions in my world

GT4854.A2S74 2016   j394.269492   C2015-907464-9
                                               C2015-907465-7

Library of Congress Cataloging-in-Publication Data

Names: Spence, Kelly, author.
Title: Cultural traditions in the Netherlands / Kelly Spence.
Description: New York, New York : Crabtree Publishing, [2016] | Series: Cultural traditions in my world | Includes index. | Description based on print version record and CIP data provided by publisher; resource not viewed.
Identifiers: LCCN 2015045084 (print) | LCCN 2015042104 (ebook) | ISBN 9781427180957 (electronic HTML) | ISBN 9780778780892 (reinforced library binding : alkaline paper) | ISBN 9780778780939 (paperback : alkaline paper)
Subjects: LCSH: Holidays--Netherlands--Juvenile literature. | Festivals--Netherlands--Juvenile literature. | Fasts and feasts--Netherlands--Juvenile literature. | Netherlands--Social life and customs--Juvenile literature.
Classification: LCC GT4854.A2 (print) | LCC GT4854.A2 S64 2016 (ebook) | DDC 394.269492--dc23
LC record available at http://lccn.loc.gov/2015045084

Crabtree Publishing Company
www.crabtreebooks.com   1-800-387-7650

Printed in Canada/022016/IH20151223

Published in Canada
Crabtree Publishing
616 Welland Ave.
St. Catharines, ON
L2M 5V6

Published in the United States
Crabtree Publishing
PMB 59051
350 Fifth Avenue, 59th Floor
New York, New York 10118

Published in the United Kingdom
Crabtree Publishing
Maritime House
Basin Road North, Hove
BN41 1WR

Published in Australia
Crabtree Publishing
3 Charles Street
Coburg North
VIC 3058

Contents

Welcome to the Netherlands

The Kingdom of the Netherlands is a flat country located in western Europe. Over 16 million people live in this small country. The official language is Dutch, but the government also recognizes a regional language from the province of Friesland called Frisian. Many Dutch people also speak English.

The Netherlands is bordered by Germany, Belgium, and the North Sea.

Amsterdam is the capital city of the Netherlands, but the government is located in a city called The Hague (above).

Culture is the common beliefs and practices shared by a group of people. A country's culture is expressed through its language, history, and religion. Most people in the Netherlands are **Christian**. The country also has small **Jewish** and **Muslim** populations.

About half of the Netherlands is located below sea level. Over hundreds of years, the Dutch have built **canals** to drain wet, marshy areas.

Special Days

The Dutch celebrate many of the same traditions as people in North America, but they often include their own unique customs. At a wedding, sweetmeats called "bridal sugar" and a spiced wine called "bride's tears" are served. After the wedding, new couples often plant lilies of the valley. These flowers symbolize "the return of happiness." As they bloom each year, the couple are reminded to celebrate their love and happiness for each other.

Did You Know?
In Dutch culture, it is common to greet family and friends with three kisses on the cheek.

A lily of the valley is a sweet-smelling flower that is native to northern Europe and Asia as well as eastern North America.

After a baby is born, it is a traditional Dutch custom to serve *beschuit met muisjes*, or "biscuits with mice." The "mice" are tiny licorice-flavored seeds. On their birthdays, boys and girls provide cake for everyone to enjoy. It is also common to congratulate the person on their birthday. Another unique Dutch tradition happens when students finish school. They hang their backpacks, along with the national flag, outside of their homes to let everyone know they have passed their exams.

Beschuit met muisjes. Special cookies to celebrate a new baby: pink for a girl and blue for a boy.

After the school year ends in June, backpacks are proudly hung outside many homes in the Netherlands.

7

Happy New Year!

Did You Know?
Wish someone a happy new year in Dutch by saying *Gelukkig nieuwjaar*!

On New Year's Eve, colorful fireworks light up the sky and festive bonfires burn brightly throughout the Netherlands. It is traditional to enjoy sweet treats like *oliebollen*, which are deep-fried donuts coated with icing sugar, and *appelflappen*, or apple fritters.

Oliebollen are often made with sweet fruits such as apples, currants, and raisins.

The brave people who take part in the New Year's Dive in Scheveningen receive orange hats and mittens. Orange is the national color of the Netherlands. The dive is followed by a hot bowl of pea soup.

The following day, some towns and villages organize events called *Nieuwjaarsduik*, or New Year's Dives. This is where people plunge into the cold North Sea, lakes, or canals. In the southern city of Scheveningen, over ten thousand people take part in this adventurous tradition.

National Tulip Day

Nationale Tulpendag, or National Tulip Day, is celebrated in mid-January. This day marks the official start of the tulip season in the Netherlands. Over 200,000 colorful tulips bloom in Dam Square in the heart of Amsterdam. The tulip is considered by many to be the unofficial national flower of the Netherlands. The flower was brought to the Netherlands by the Turkish in the 1500s.

Thousands of people visit Dam Square and pick a free tulip on National Tulip Day.

A boat covered in purple flowers sails through the area of Westland in South Holland.

Later in the spring, many people visit Keukenhof Gardens which showcase over eight hundred different kinds of tulips. In many cities throughout the year, flower parades, or *bloemencorsos*, feature beautiful floats covered in blossoms. Some parades even take place on the canals.

Did You Know?
Nicknamed the "flower shop of the world," the Netherlands is the largest exporter of tulips in the world. Each year, the country exports over three billion bulbs.

Carnival

Carnival is a holiday that is celebrated in many places around the world. In the Netherlands, this festive holiday is largely celebrated in the southern provinces. It is celebrated for three days leading up to the Christian season of **Lent**. Lent takes place about six weeks before Easter Sunday.

Did You Know?
As a fun tradition, some towns change their names during Carnival. The town of 's-Hertogenbosch, for example, changes its name to Oeteldonk!

Colorful floats travel through the streets of Oldenzaal during one of the Netherland's largest Carnival parades.

The *polonaise* is a popular dance during Carnival.

Carnival kicks off with a parade led by the Carnival Prince. He is greeted with three cheers of "*alaaf!*" which is a traditional Carnival greeting. Most people celebrate by eating, drinking, and dancing in colorful costumes. In some areas, there are special Carnival parties and children's parades.

Carnival celebrations are enjoyed by Dutch people of all ages.

Easter

Easter celebrations in the Netherlands are very similar to those in North America. This holiday is based on the Christian celebration of Jesus Christ's **crucifixion** on Good Friday and His **resurrection** on Easter Sunday. Many people attend church services on these days.

Did You Know?
In the town of Ootmarsum on Easter Sunday, eight men wearing wide-brimmed hats lead a procession through the town singing Easter songs. This traditional celebration ends with a bonfire.

Worshipers gather for a Good Friday service at a church in Amsterdam.

At Easter, Dutch families enjoy foods such as an Easter bread called *paasstol*. This bread is filled with raisins, nuts, and **marzipan**.

Not all families celebrate Easter as a religious holiday. Leading up to Easter, many children paint eggs. On Easter morning, children look forward to treats and gifts brought by the *Paashaas*, or Easter Hare. They also take part in egg hunts.

In many homes, bouquets of willow branches are hung with wooden eggs as decorations at Easter.

King's Day

The birthday of the **reigning** king or queen has been celebrated as a holiday since 1885.

On King's Day, the streets of cities and towns across the Netherlands are filled with *oranjegekte*, meaning "orange madness." Orange is the country's national color. On this much-loved holiday, the entire country celebrates King Willem-Alexander's birthday. As part of the celebration, the royal family visits a different city each year.

In Amsterdam, a parade makes its way along the canals. A huge street sale known as *vrijmarkt*, or free market, also takes place on King's Day in many cities. Anyone can set up a stall and sell their used items. Children celebrate the holiday by playing traditional Dutch games, such as *koekhappen*, in which participants try to eat a sweet pastry hanging from a string without using their hands.

It is common to see orange ribbons added to the country's flag to celebrate King's Day.

Did You Know?
Queen Beatrice, King Willem-Alexander's mother, reigned in the Netherlands until 2013. Until then, King's Day was known as Queen's Day.

Even children set up their own stalls to participate in *vrijmarkt*.

Days of Remembrance

May 4 is a day of remembrance in the Netherlands. This **solemn** day honors the Dutch who have died in war and peacekeeping missions since World War II. Each year, a special remembrance ceremony takes place at Dam Square in Amsterdam. Flags fly at half-mast on this day as a sign of respect. At 8 p.m., the entire country observes two minutes of silence.

During the Remembrance Day ceremony, King Willem-Alexander and his wife Queen Maxima lay a memorial wreath.

People ride on a tank from World War II during a Remembrance Day parade.

Liberation Day, or Freedom Day, is celebrated on May 5. It marks the end of the five-year German **occupation** of the Netherlands during World War II. This national holiday is celebrated every five years. Many cities host free outdoor concerts and parades.

Did You Know?
In 2015, a special celebration marked the 70th anniversary of the Dutch liberation. Many services honored the foreign soldiers who helped free the Dutch from German rule.

National Mill Day

National Mill Day is celebrated in the Netherlands during the second weekend of May. Mills have been an important part of the country's history. For hundreds of years they were used to produce food and materials, as well as to keep the land dry. Today, **windmills** are a popular tourist attraction across the country.

Did You Know?
Before telephones and the Internet, the position of a windmill's **sails** was often used to communicate messages across long distances. Messages could be an announcement of a birth or death, or also a call for help.

Many windmills are connected by winding bike paths in the Dutch countryside.

Wheat is a grain that is ground to make flour. Flour is used to make bread and many other foods.

Mills are often decorated with flowers and flags on National Mill Day.

On Mill Day, 950 windmills and **watermills** are opened to celebrate this unique part of Dutch **heritage**. Many families take part in traditional activities, such as making pancakes and bread from grain that is freshly ground by a mill. Many people travel by bicycle to visit different mills. Each year more than 100,000 people take part in Mill Day festivities.

Ascension Day and Pentecost

Ascension Day and Pentecost, also known as Whit Sunday, are traditionally Christian holidays celebrated in the Netherlands. Ascension Day is celebrated forty days after Easter and marks Jesus's rise to heaven.

This painting by the famous Dutch artist Rembrandt shows Jesus ascending to heaven.

Did You Know? Traditionally on Ascension Day, it was believed that walking barefoot in the dewy grass provided special healing powers.

Pentecost falls ten days after Ascension Day and symbolizes the Holy Spirit's **descent** from heaven. In the northern and eastern parts of the country, many people spend both these holidays going for early-morning walks or bicycle rides. A popular children's celebration for Whit Sunday in the eastern and southern provinces includes dressing in spring colors and dancing around a tall, decorated pole that has ribbons attached to it. During this time, some schools close for a few weeks.

Cuckoo flowers have traditionally been used as Pentecost flowers because they bloom during this time of the year.

Flag Day

In early June, the seaside town of Scheveningen hosts *Vlaggetjesdag*, or Flag Day. This street festival has been celebrated for over 60 years and marks the first catch of the herring season. Herring is a silver fish found in the salty waters of the North Sea. The Dutch have eaten raw herring for over 600 years.

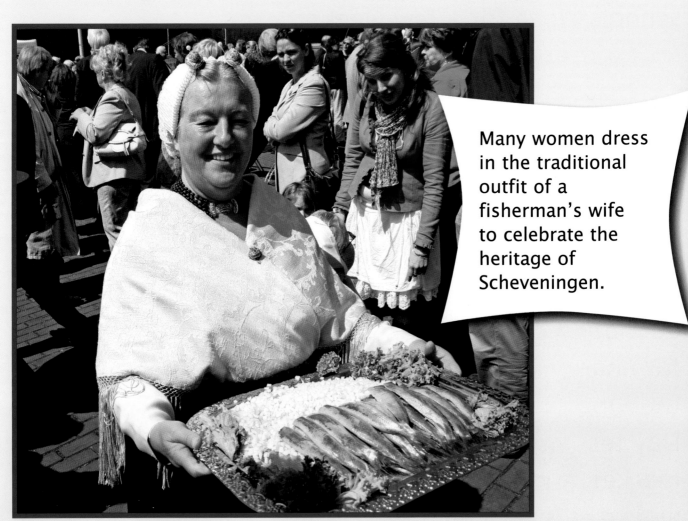

Many women dress in the traditional outfit of a fisherman's wife to celebrate the heritage of Scheveningen.

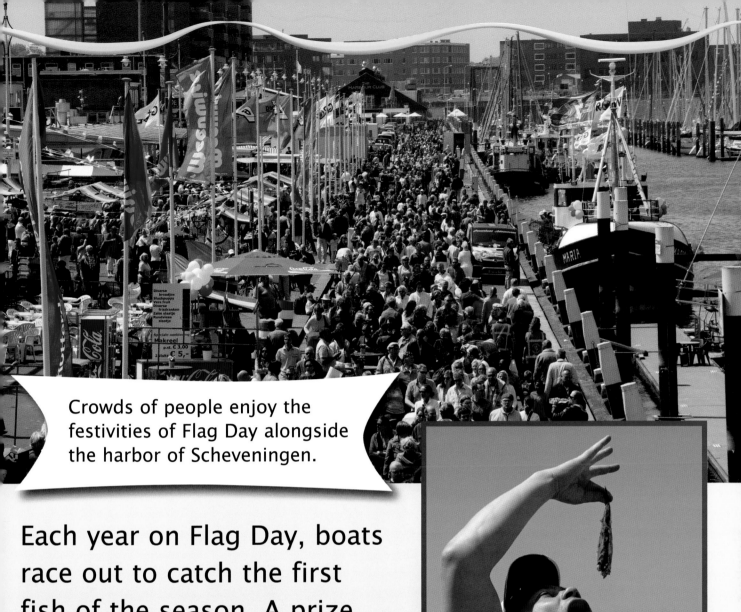

Crowds of people enjoy the festivities of Flag Day alongside the harbor of Scheveningen.

Each year on Flag Day, boats race out to catch the first fish of the season. A prize is awarded to the first boat that returns. The first barrel of herring is traditionally auctioned off to raise money for charity, and presented to the king or queen. Other flag Day festivities include a street market, a moustache contest, and games for children.

Did You Know?
The traditional way to eat raw herring is to hold the fish by its tail, dip it in chopped onions, and then take a big bite.

25

St. Martin's Day

On November 11, the Dutch celebrate *Sint-Maarten*, or St. Martin's Day. This holiday is in memory of the **monk**, St. Martin of Tours. He is remembered for his kindness toward strangers.

While St. Martin served in the Roman army, he held onto his Christian values. A famous story, shown in this painting, tells of his generosity toward a beggar. When St. Martin saw the poor man shivering, he selflessly tore off his cloak and gave it to him.

Did You Know?
Traditionally, St. Martin's day lanterns were carved out of turnips or beets, and attached to a string.

During the evening on St. Martin's Day, children go door to door carrying brightly lit homemade or store-bought paper lanterns. At each home, the children sing traditional songs in exchange for treats. One popular song includes the words:

Sint Maarten Sint Maarten
The cows have tails
The girls wear skirts
Sint Martinus is coming

Sinterklaas

Children across the country look forward to the arrival of Sinterklaas in mid-November. The legend of Sinterklaas is based on a Turkish **bishop**, St. Nicholas, who is remembered for his kindness toward children. Sinterklaas arrives in the Netherlands by steamship from Spain. He is dressed in red robes and rides a white horse.

Most towns have a holiday parade that features Sinterklaas on his horse.

Children often leave a carrot for Sinterklaas's horse.

Did You Know?
If children have not been well-behaved during the past year, they might find a lump of coal or bag of salt in their shoe, instead of presents!

On December 5, before bed, boys and girls leave their shoes out to be filled with sweets and presents from Sinterklaas. It is also common for friends and family members to give secret gifts, often with a funny poem attached. The poems are often riddles and everyone tries to guess who gave each gift.

Sweets such as spicy, licorice-flavored cookies called *peppernoot*, and chocolate letters are enjoyed during this holiday.

Christmas

Throughout December, Christmas markets spring up all over the Netherlands. Vendors set up stalls to sell goods and tasty treats, such as *stroopwafel*, which is made of two thin waffles with a layer of caramel spread in between.

Stroopwafel

Christmas markets also celebrate the holiday with festive light displays.

On December 26, many people go ice skating on the canals, if the water is frozen.

Did You Know?
The Dutch wish one another a Merry Christmas by saying *Vrolijk Kerstfeest*!

In the Netherlands, Christmas falls over both December 25 and 26. After the gift-giving festivities of Sinterklaas, the focus of Christmas itself is spending time with family. At Christmas dinner, a traditional turkey is often accompanied by *kerststol*, or Christmas bread (right).

Glossary

bishop A high-ranking member in the Christian church

canals Waterways built by people for boats to travel on or to drain or irrigate land

Christian A follower of Jesus Christ and member of the Christian church

crucifixion The act of putting a person to death by nailing their hands and feet to a cross

descent The act of coming down from a higher place

heritage Something passed down from the past

Jewish Describing a follower of Judaism who believes in one God and follows the Old Testament of the Bible

Lent In the Christian church, a period of forty days leading up to Easter during which something is often given up

marzipan A sweet paste made from almonds and sugar

monk A male religious figure

Muslim A follower of the Islam religion

occupation Taking control and power of an area

reign To rule, usually as a king or queen

resurrection The rising of Jesus Christ from the dead

sails Pieces of fabric stretched over a frame that are used to catch wind.

solemn Serious

watermill A mill powered by water moving through a waterwheel

windmill A structure with sails, powered by the wind, used to generate power to grind materials such as grain, flour, and wood

Index